THE

CHRISTIAN ENDEAVOR

BUILDING

Its History and Surroundings

BY
AMOS R. WELLS

First Fruits Press
Wilmore, Kentucky
c2015

First Fruits Press
The Academic Open Press of Asbury Theological Seminary
204 N. Lexington Ave., Wilmore, KY 40390
859-858-2236
first.fruits@asburyseminary.edu
asbury.to/firstfruits

THE
CHRISTIAN ENDEAVOR
BUILDING

Its History and Surroundings

BY

AMOS R. WELLS

BOSTON AND CHICAGO
UNITED SOCIETY OF CHRISTIAN ENDEAVOR

The Fireplace of the Clark Room.

Over the mantelpiece is the portrait of Dr. Clark. Below it are three loving-cups given to Dr. Clark at important anniversaries.

Dr. Clark at His Desk.

This room is the central point of Christian Endeavor. Many unique memorials hang on the walls.

THE CHRISTIAN ENDEAVOR BUILDING

I. The History of the Building.

THE first Christian Endeavor headquarters was Dr. Clark's study in Portland, Me., whence emanated, after the founding of the society on February 2, 1881, the strong purpose and fervent zeal which carried the new movement so far. Two years later, when Dr. Clark became pastor of Phillips Church in South Boston, the headquarters was transferred to his study there. From these two "headquarters" came the first newspaper articles about Christian Endeavor, and the first Christian Endeavor book, "Children and the Church."

Four years after the founding of the society, in July, 1885, the United Society of Christian Endeavor was established, and Rev. S. W. Adriance was chosen general secretary. After a few weeks of service, he was induced by his church to resign the new work, and his place was filled by George M. Ward, now Rev. George M. Ward, D. D., LL. D., ex-president of Rollins College and of Wells College. His office in Boston was the first headquarters of the United Society.

"This office," Dr. Ward writes me, "was located at 14 Beacon Street, on the ground floor in the back of the salesroom of the Massachusetts Bible Society, where the Bibles were on exhibition and sale. I had no office associates at the outset; later I was assisted by a stenographer.

"You see, my 'office' wasn't an office. I had merely the opportunity to put a table and later a desk at the rear end of the said Bible rooms. I thought we had progressed considerably when I allowed myself the luxury of a roll-top desk. We were there about half a year, and moved to 50 Bromfield Street, in the fall of 1886, because the work had outgrown our surroundings."

Compare that first office with the splendidly equipped building which now occupies the summit of Beacon Hill and you will have a concrete evidence of what these thirty-three years, only a third of a century, have done for Christian Endeavor.

At 50 Bromfield.

My own memories begin with Christian Endeavor's second headquarters, 50 Bromfield Street, where the United Society had spent five years. There I found *The Golden Rule* and the United Society at the

5

Looking from the Roof of the Christian Endeavor Building Southward.
The old buildings in the foreground will go some day, doubtless, to make the State House Park, and then we shall have nothing between us and the famous Boston Common.

close of 1891. The entire establishment occupied three rooms on the fourth floor. The rooms were not large, but each of them housed four or five workers. The editorial room, I remember, had my desk next to the window; and I was glad to occupy a strategic position with reference to fresh air. Next to me was Miss Wilcox, the news editor, and next to her was Mr. Kelly, the literary editor. Dr. Clark was favored with a cubby-hole partitioned off in one corner, where Dr. Dickinson and Dr. Hill often withdrew for a conference on the state of Christian Endeavor in general and this paper in particular. I am rather vague about the location of Messrs. Baer, Shaw, and Graff, but they tucked themselves away somewhere. I remember the pleasure I had in that stuffy little office surveying the first illustrated number of our paper, that for January 7, 1892. It contained only two pictures, very woodeny wood engravings of President William R. Harper and Mrs. Alice May Scudder; but oh, how proud we were of them! I remember, too, how exalted I was with my first bit of work for the United Society, a pamphlet of programmes and hints for union meetings.

At 47 Franklin.

The rooms at 50 Bromfield Street, however, soon became palpably and suffocatingly too small for the entire staff, so that early in 1892 occurred the first and only separation between the Golden Rule Company and the United Society. We, *The Golden Rule*, moved to a floor near the top of 47 Franklin Street, while the United Society remained behind and, Dr. Clark, as editor-in-chief of the one and president of the other, vibrated between the two establishments. It was observed, however, that his Franklin Street office was seldom occupied, and occupied for only brief periods. The fact is that the heavy presses at work

on several floors of that building caused it to sway with a very marine motion, and I knew what seasickness was long before I made my first voyage to Europe. Dr. Clark is a seasoned sailor, but he could not stand 47 Franklin Street. Our own press did its full share toward the quaking. We had rough little offices with thin board partitions, but each of us had an office to himself or herself, so that we felt ourselves well up in the world.

At 646 Washington.

Our next move, however, which came at the end of that same eventful year, 1892, sent us to far better quarters. To be sure, we were farther from the centre of things, at 646 Washington Street, but the United Society and the Golden Rule Company were together again, we were on the same floor, and each of us had a little more room than before, so that we felt ourselves very fortunate.

We were in the John H. Pray Building, over the carpet-store where Secretary Shaw had formerly "clerked it." Our little offices were still fenced off with board partitions, and they must have looked quite primitive to Cyrus H. K. Curtis when that great publisher paid us a visit one day; but we had glorious times there, and did a lot of work.

I remember that my window looked out on an alley, with a chocolate-factory on one side and a Chinese theatre on the other; and it was impossible to tell which was worse, the nauseating odor of the one or the deafening and continuous din of the other. We could not corral the smell, but we did get a policeman up into my room and enter formal and effective complaint against the Chinese gongs.

It was at 646 Washington that Miss Wilcox left us for her happy married life, and her place was taken by that efficient editor and brilliant writer, William T. Ellis, who

6

has since made such a name for himself. Dr. Ellis (not then a Doctor of Laws, however) put in all his service at 646 Washington Street, and so did his successor, Rev. Frederic S. Boody, the able young Baptist whose poor health compelled him after a few months to drop the work so admirably begun. His place was taken by Dr. John F. Cowan, who came to us early in 1898, and who is still connected with the paper as the beloved writer of the Sunday-school comments.

At Tremont Temple.

A year later, in January, 1899, the United Society and the Golden Rule Company removed to the home we occupied for so long, Tremont Temple. Here we used the greater part of the sixth floor, while the editorial rooms of this paper were on the seventh floor. In Tremont Temple Secretary Baer, when he left us for the Presbyterian Board of Home Missions, was succeeded by Secretary Vogt; and the latter, when he followed Secretary Baer in the same position, was succeeded by Secretary Shaw. Tremont Temple also saw the end of Mr. George B. Graff's long service as publication manager, the shorter service of Mr. Arthur E. Watkins, and the beginning of the work of Mr. A. J. Shartle, who came to us from his efficient service as Pennsylvania's field-secretary. Tremont Temple

was also the headquarters of our first field-secretary, the beloved Clarence E. Eberman, a truly apostolic worker, who died in the course of a Christian Endeavor journey.

In Tremont Temple we celebrated the twenty-fifth and thirtieth anniversaries of Christian Endeavor with notable meetings, held an All-New-England Convention with striking features, and inaugurated many Christian Endeavor plans of far-reaching importance. The weekly prayer meetings of the office force and the occasional jolly social gatherings made those rooms very dear to us.

At 31 Mt. Vernon.

Nevertheless we were very glad, in June, 1914, to move back upon Beacon Hill where were the first headquarters, for this time we went into our own buildings. The two brick houses, 31 Mt. Vernon Street and 75 Hancock Street, were occupied, the first by the United Society and the second by THE CHRISTIAN ENDEAVOR WORLD. They are quaint, old-fashioned buildings, aged seventy-five years, and were handsome residences in their day.

We filled both buildings from cellar to garret, and they were just a good fit. A "Bridge of Sighs" connected the two buildings. Here we were very happy, and carried on some of the most important Chris-

Looking Eastward from the Roof of the Christian Endeavor Building in Boston.

The Massachusetts State House is in the foreground. The gilded dome is the famous "Hub" of Dr. Holmes's fancy, which has given Boston its popular name. The tower in the distance is that of the Custom House, the highest edifice in New England.

tian Endeavor "campaigns" and other enterprises. Here, too, the officers of the United Society, one after the other, were laid aside temporarily with a series of severe hospital experiences, but came out of them in some respects better than new. Here also, of course, the Building fund was completed, and the plans for Christian Endeavor's permanent headquarters were carefully formed. By July, 1918, we had moved into the new Building, which was dedicated with a series of meetings of trustees, field-secretaries, and other leading Endeavorers, on July 30—August 1. From that date we reckon the new era of Christian Endeavor.

At 41 Mt. Vernon.

The Building is six stories high, with a basement equal in usefulness to another story. It is built to the full height allowed on Beacon Hill. The ground area of the Building is 4,200 square feet, its height, 70 feet. The floors above the first are each divided into fourteen offices. The basement and first story are of Indiana limestone, and

The Entrance Hall.

The entrance to the Christian Endeavor Building is a beautiful one. It is finished in marble, faces a marble stairway, and shows through large glass doors the Clark Christian Endeavor Museum on the right and the United Society Bookstore and Bookkeeping Department on the left the upper stories are brick with limestone trimmings. In perfect harmony with the State House and with most of the buildings on Beacon Hill, the style of the building is early Colonial. The general effect is dignified and very pleasing. The architects, Messrs. Brainerd and Leeds and O. A. Thayer, have to their credit a number of especially fine buildings, including the Ford Building on Beacon Hill and the new building of the New England Historic Genealogical Society near it.

The builders are Messrs. W. A. and H. A. Root. Mr. H. A. Root, Mr. McCutcheon of his firm, and Messrs. Brainerd, Leeds, and Thayer, the architects, are all old-time Endeavorers. The C. E. monogram is over the handsome mahogany doorway as part of the beautiful pillared entrance. It is also conspicuous in the stone-work of the cornice, while the letters, "C. E.," appear in the stone lintels of the windows.

Entering, we find the hallways charmingly light and most tastefully decorated. The floors are of terrazo and marble. In the vestibule is a bronze tablet whose words are by Dr. Clark:

ERECTED
TO THE GLORY OF GOD
BY THE GIFTS OF MORE THAN
ONE HUNDRED THOUSAND
CHRISTIAN ENDEAVORERS
AND THEIR FRIENDS
IN EVERY LAND
AND DEDICATED
TO THE TRAINING
OF YOUNG PEOPLE
FOR THE SERVICE OF CHRIST
AND THEIR FELLOW MEN

In the reception hall is another bronze tablet:

CHRISTIAN ENDEAVOR
BUILDING
CORNER STONE LAID JULY 18, 1917
BUILDING COMMITTEE
FRANCIS E. CLARK

HOWARD B. GROSE   DANIEL A. POLING
WILLIAM SHAW   JACOB J. ARAKELYAN
ALVIN J. SHARTLE   AMOS R. WELLS
JAMES L. HILL   ROBERT P. ANDERSON

ARCHITECTS
BRAINERD AND LEEDS AND O. A. THAYER
BUILDERS
W. A. AND H. A. ROOT, INC.

At the right of the reception hall, separated from it by glass doors, is the Clark Memorial Hall, a large room in perfect Colonial style, with simple but elegant ornaments. Over the fireplace is a large portrait of Dr. Clark, and below it a handsome clock and two candlesticks presented by Mr. Asa Turner, 3d, of Iowa. At the farther end of the room, on the low platform, is the very desk on which the first Christian Endeavor constitution was

signed in the Williston parsonage, Portland, Me., on that famous second of February, 1881.

Around the walls are many glass cases in which are displayed scores of memorials of Christian Endeavor in all lands, brilliant banners from many nations, bright badges, the historic gavels of many conventions, photographs galore, and numberless other souvenirs of Christian Endeavor, including the unequalled collection of Dr. Clark, and the splendid collection given to the Christian Endeavor Museum by Merritt B. Holley. The cabinets and drawers below the cases are for files of Christian Endeavor papers, notable programmes, reports, Christian Endeavor books and pamphlets, and other printed and written records of our society.

Across the hall from the Clark room is the book-store which Mr. Shartle has fitted up most effectively for the display and sale of the more than one thousand books, pamphlets, and other articles which crowd the United Society's catalogue of workers' helps.

Back of this is a room given up to the United Society bookkeepers, while the space in the rear is a large and well-lighted room devoted to the circulation clerks of THE CHRISTIAN ENDEAVOR WORLD, with separate offices for Mr. Charles S. Brown, the circulation manager, and Miss Bradford, the bookkeeper.

The extensive basement is occupied with the United Society shipping-room, the shipping-room of THE CHRISTIAN ENDEAVOR WORLD, and the well-planned composing-room of THE CHRISTIAN ENDEAVOR WORLD,

The Marble Tablet in the
Entrance Hall.

9

whose able foreman is Ernest Acker, ex-captain in the State Guard and ex-mayor of Revere. No part of the busy building is busier than the basement.

Ascending the beautiful white marble stairway to the second story, we find the hallways lined with collections of photographs from all Christian Endeavor lands, illustrating many phases of the society's activity. Visitors will turn first to the President's room at the southwest corner, and will find it handsomely fitted out with mahogany furniture and a plain rug of rich green, while the walls carry many memorials of Christian Endeavor. Dr. Clark's office will be in the future as in the

TIAN ENDEAVOR WORLD, for he is the tireless and most capable general secretary of the one and the energetic publisher of the other. Across the hall is the bright room of the advertising department of the paper, where the field representative of the United Society and THE CHRISTIAN ENDEAVOR WORLD, Mr. Clarence C. Hamilton, former field-secretary of Ohio and Y. M. C. A. war secretary, has his abode.

The three offices remaining are those of the present writer, managing editor of the paper since December, 1891, and his two associates, Mr. Arthur W. Kelly (of even longer service) and Rev. R. P. Anderson. My own desk is prized by me because of

Dr. Poling between Journeys.

The walls of his office show many souvenirs of his Christian Endeavor journeys to Europe.

past the very heart of Christian Endeavor.

Passing down a private hallway past the rooms of Dr. Clark's and Dr. Poling's secretaries, we come to the beautiful little office of our associate president, with its flat-top desk, and its tokens on the walls of the splendid and varied work in which he is engaged. Next to Dr. Clark's office on the Joy Street side, going through the room of Mr. Shartle's secretary, we reach the quiet abode of our busy publication manager, never so busy as now. Mr. Shartle has chutes leading from his office to the store and the shipping-room, and is in close touch with all branches of the work.

Secretary Shaw's office, next in order, is the connecting link between the domain of the United Society and that of THE CHRIS-

long association with my work, and because previously it was the desk used by John Willis Baer. Each editor has at his disposal a copy chute connecting him with the printing-office two floors below.

Two rooms remain to complete our Christian Endeavor list, one occupied by the office exchange telephone and the statistical secretary of the United Society, and a room above it on the third floor which is the office of Field-Secretary Gates and Alumni Superintendent Vandersall.

Our Tenants.

The rest of the third floor is rented by the New England Lord's Day League and the well-known publishers, Small, May-

10

Looking West from the Top of the Christian Endeavor Building.
The Charles River is seen in the distance.

nard, and Company. *The Atlantic Monthly,* Boston's famous magazine so intimately bound up with all that is best in American literature, occupies the fourth and fifth floors with its happily growing activities, including the publication of *The House Beautiful* and *Littell's Living Age.* The sixth floor is occupied by a leading concern, the Greenleaf Advertising Agency.

The roof is tiled, the cornice furnishing a high balustrade, and from this, the summit of Beacon Hill, a wonderfully beautiful and meaningful panorama is spread out —the harbor of the Tea Party, with its shipping and islands, Dorchester Heights with its memories of Washington and the siege of Boston, Boston Common and the Public Garden, the Blue Hills in the distance, the Back Bay with the great classic buildings of the Institute of Technology on its banks, Cambridge with the towers of Harvard and of Mount Auburn and with Lexington and Concord beyond, and to the north the superb Custom House tower and beyond it Bunker Hill Monument. No building in any city of America commands a nobler sweep of historic scenery than can be viewed from the roof of our Christian Endeavor Headquarters. We hope that its physical outlook will be equalled—and even excelled—by its spiritual views, and that from this summit will go forth inspiring influences to all the nations of the globe.

The Building Project Launched.

The Christian Endeavor Building project was launched at the enthusiastic International Convention held in Baltimore in July, 1905. At once the Endeavorers rose to the idea. I have never witnessed a more zealous and eager spirit than was

Looking Northward from the Top of the Building.
The view is toward Bunker Hill and is a magnificent one, crowded with historic associations.

11

The Speaker's Stand in the Clark Room.

The desk is the one on which, in Dr. Clark's study in Portland, the first Christian Endeavor constitution was written and signed. A page of the original in Dr. Clark's handwriting is here displayed.

shown by the union officers' rally when William Shaw, then the United Society treasurer, announced the plan, which had just received the approval of the trustees.

I could hardly keep back the tears of joy as from a gallery I looked down upon that crowd of State leaders. All over the house they were springing to their feet. "I second the motion for Pennsylvania!" cried one. "And I for Massachusetts!" shouted another. "Arkansas wants to be counted in!" "Missouri will do her share!" Thus it went on, dozens shouting at once. Over and over they asked to be allowed to pledge

actual sums, but those in charge of the movement did not wish that at the start. Nevertheless Professor James Lewis Howe, that ardent trustee from the Southern Presbyterian Church, managed to get in the first gift from an individual. The Christ's Lutheran Endeavorers of Baltimore made the first society gift of twenty-five cents a member. Ohio and Illinois simultaneously made the first gifts from State unions. Yet where all were equally ready it is invidious to mention names.

The Building was proposed as a memorial of the first quarter-century of the ex-

12

istence of the Christian Endeavor Society, which was celebrated by the Baltimore Convention. The average gift of twenty-five cents a member, one cent for each year of Christian Endeavor's life, was asked from the Endeavorers (and ten cents each from the Juniors). A strong set of resolutions from the trustees indorsed the plan, which was also commended by letters from scores of eminent Christian leaders. A thoroughgoing set of explanatory circulars was prepared and sent to all the societies and the campaign was on.

Early Gifts.

A steady stream of quarters came in. "Why not put the average at fifty cents a member?" wrote a prison Endeavorer; and from his scanty resources he promised a dollar. Another prison Endeavorer, who had overcome the tobacco habit since joining the prison society, had no money except the prison allowance of twenty-five cents a month for tobacco, but gladly sent fifty cents. The first gift from a Floating society was $1.50 from the Endeavorers of the United States Flagship Maine. Portuguese Juniors of Honolulu sent $2.50. Dr. Pettee sent early gifts from Japan, including four dollars from the children of the Okayama Orphanage. Thirty-three Indian Endeavorers of North Dakota sent $8.25. Gifts began to come in from hundreds of workers and societies all over the United States.

Treasurer Shaw was the first field campaigner. He made, in the fall of 1905, a two-months tour in the interest of the Memorial Fund, visiting nine States and Ontario, and finding everywhere an abundant enthusiasm which his earnest eloquence did much to increase.

Organizing the Project.

In the fall of 1905 an International Committee was formed for the Building. Its President was Hon. Henry B. F. Macfarland, Commissioner of the District of Columbia; its Treasurer was William Shaw; its Secretary, Amos R. Wells; and its Finance Committee was Hon. Samuel B. Capen, LL. D., President of the American Board, Hon. John L. Bates, LL. D., Ex-governor of Massachusetts, and Henry W. Peabody, a leading Boston merchant. Governor Bates has given interested and faithful service upon this committee through all the money-raising campaigns. Dr. Capen was very active in the work until his lamented death, when he was succeeded by William Shaw, LL. D., the general secretary of the United Society. On the death of Mr. Peabody his successor was the well-known paper manufacturer, Col. Edward H. Haskell, a man of many good works who has shown great and steady interest in the Building. Thus the Congregational, Methodist, and Baptist denominations have been constantly represented on the Finance Committee. In addition, Treasurer Lathrop

Dr. Clark Reading His Address at the Dedication Exercises on the Roof.

13

The Clark Room, Looking toward Mt. Vernon Street.

and his successor, Treasurer Shartle, have served on the Finance Committee *ex officio*. Scores of leading men in the United States and in all parts of the world accepted positions on the general committee, which was truly international and representative.

Unique Offerings.

With such backing the cause of the Building boomed. A generous gift came from the Armenian Endeavorers of Erzroum, Asia Minor. The Endeavorers of the North China Mission sent a contribution in gold. The native Endeavorers of Kusaie in the Caroline Islands, recently made homeless by a terrible hurricane, sent $12.50. Six dollars came from the Endeavorers of Cairo, Egypt. The Endeavorers of Cachoeira, Brazil, gave $12—the first contribution from South America. Germany's first offering was $250.

From a logging-camp society in Alabama we received $12. Spain started its fund with $35, and Sweden with $25. Two boys in Japan sent a collection of Japanese stamps to be sold for the Building. The Chinese Endeavorers of Fall River, Mass., sent a generous sum. Denmark's two societies gave twenty-five crowns. At the consecration meeting of the Japan union convention of 1906 they made a Building offering of twenty yen. Rev. R. M. Cole, of Bitlis, Turkey, sent $12.10 from his family and ten Armenian orphans who earned the money they sent.

Boston held a Building banquet attended by three hundred Endeavorers, including thirty-five ministers. Hungary made a "jubilee gift" to the "Clark House." The Christian Endeavor girls of Madrid, Spain, sent $10, mostly earned by needlework. These are all notes from the first year's giving. At the end of that year the banner society was the Tenth Presbyterian of Philadelphia, whose generous Endeavorers had given to the Building $250.

Boston Selected.

It was uncertain at first where the Christian Endeavor Building would be located. Washington, New York, Philadelphia, Chicago, and St. Louis each had ardent advocates. A canvass of Christian Endeavor leaders over the entire country, however, showed a decided preference for the city identified most closely with Christian Endeavor from the beginning, and this choice of Boston was ratified by the trustees at their meeting in connection with the National Christian Endeavor Institute held in New York City in February, 1906.

An early plan for raising money was by the sale of Building coupons, each standing for the gift of a dollar, put up in twenty-five-dollar books. Engraved certificates were given to all contributors, showing their "shares" in the Building at twenty-five cents a share.

Other Notable Contributions.

The giving of the second year, 1906-7, had some picturesque features. The East Gate Juniors of Madura, India, the average income of whose fathers was $5 a

14

month, sent $2. "Purchase anything with this money for your building," they wrote in Tamil. A society in Leavenworth, Kan., made up of old soldiers of the Civil War, gave $7.75. Endeavorers in the island of Trinidad sent $40 to the fund as soon as they heard about it.

The Urumia union in Persia gave $15.65. Some Italian Endeavorers in Newark, N. J., sent a gift. The Endeavorers of the Marshall Islands, forbidden by the German government to take up more than two general collections a year (and these must be at stated times), nevertheless made out of their poverty private gifts amounting to $80.70, and actually sent part of their clothing, twenty-three mats, of which Mr. Shaw made picturesque and effective use in his many appeals for the Building, finally selling them at from $3 to $100 each.

Other notable gifts during the year came from some lepers in Norway; from some Juniors in Pennsylvania who went without Christmas presents to get the money; from Germany ($450); from the British union; from the four societies in Marash, Turkey; from New South Wales Juniors ($90); from Jaffna, Ceylon ($10); from Hungary ($100); from South Africa

Our Front Door.
Notice the Christian Endeavor monogram in a beautiful scroll above the door.
The design of the entire entrance is dignified and charming.

A Homelike Entrance.

The offices of Dr. Clark, Dr. Poling, and Mr. Shartle are shut off from the elevator corridor and connected by a private corridor, through this door.

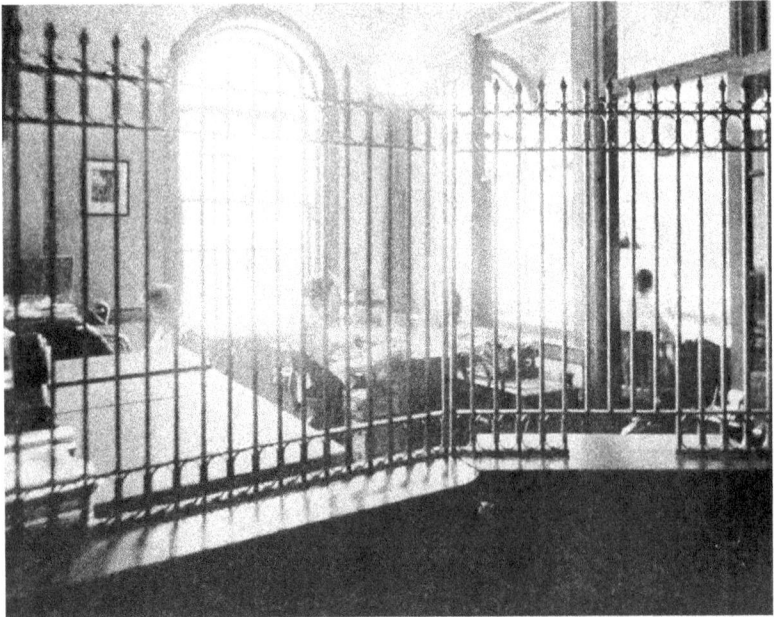

The United Society's Counting-room.

Through a handsome grating we get a glimpse of clerks busied with the financial records of Mr. Shartle's department.

($103); from Samoa and the Fiji Islands
($220); from ten societies in Brazil
($114.80); and $105 from the Andover,
Mass., union,—William Shaw's,—every
society contributing.

In the fall of 1906 Treasurer Shaw made
another Christian Endeavor journey of
more than eight thousand miles, largely in
the interests of the Building. He met with
hearty co-operation everywhere.

The "Old Guard" Steps In.

By January, 1907, $36,419 had been
raised for the Building. New York City
stood at the head of the city unions with
its gift of $1,000; Germany had given
more than any other country. Later, Australia captured this honor.

The International Convention at Seattle
in July, 1907, put new heart into the
Building campaign with its large pledges
from members of the "Old Guard" of
Christian Endeavor. At this convention
the "Builders' Union" was formed, with
"shares" at $5 each, the Christian En-
deavor alumni being especially appealed to.

In the fall of 1907 the newly chosen
superintendent of the Builders' Union, Rev.
R. P. Anderson, came to this country from
his successful missionary work in Scandi-
navia, and ever since then he has given
much time and whole-hearted labor to the
Building project, though when Dr. Cowan

fell ill he succeeded him (June, 1908) as
news editor of THE CHRISTIAN ENDEAVOR
WORLD.

By the end of the third year (July,
1908) the Building fund, cash and pledges,
had become $71,573. During the year
nearly $1,000 came from Australian En-
deavorers, and nearly $300 from the Boer
Endeavorers of South Africa.

The District of Columbia union was the
first to pledge the entire amount (500
shares) apportioned to it by the Builders'
Union.

In May, 1909, a step toward the Building was taken by the purchase of a lot at
the corner of Huntington and Longwood
Avenues, Boston, nearly half an acre, a
part of which is occupied by an apartment-
house. It was afterwards decided that
this location is too far from the centre of
Boston, and the United Society still holds
the lot, which has considerably increased
in value. Including the value of this lot,
pledges, and cash, the Building fund in
May, 1909, amounted to $80,000.

At the International Convention in St.
Paul, July of that year, the first tentative
pictures of the Building were shown. In
December, 1909, a large number of
"banks," each to hold three dollars in
dimes, were distributed through the union
officers and brought in about $5,000. Early
in 1910, during the absence of the United
Society officers attending the World's

General Secretary Shaw Planning Something New for Christian Endeavor.
The furnishings of this room were provided by the generous gifts of the
Junior Christian Endeavorers of Missouri.

17

The Clark Room at Christian Endeavor Headquarters.

We are looking out into the entrance hall. The walls are lined with glass cases filled with the most interesting memorials of Christian Endeavor history. The room is beautifully furnished in Colonial style, and has a most homelike and pleasing air.

Christian Endeavor Convention in Agra, India, an urgent series of editorials in this paper gained $5,200 for the Building.

In May, 1910, when Dr. Clark and Secretary Shaw spoke in Minneapolis, members of the "Old Guard" of Christian Endeavor quietly handed them an envelope containing $1,403 in cash and pledges for the Building. That same month Miss Flora D. Longenheld gave $400 because Secretary Blecher, of the German Christian Endeavor union, had helped to find two other persons of her family name. By July, 1910, five years after the movement was started, Mr. Anderson was able to report (including pledges) a fund of $93,618.

The Campaign of 1911.

1911 was a great year for the Building. By the end of January we had in cash and pledges $97,000. Then a nation-wide campaign was inaugurated. The beloved field-secretary, Rev. C. H. Hubbell, D. D., made tours for the Building in Tennessee and Pennsylvania. Field-Secretary W. D. Howell went to New Hampshire and Maine. Poling campaigned through Western States and Canada. Shaw made a vigorous canvass of New York cities, decking himself in Turkish fez, Burmese shirt, Marshall Islands skirt (mat), and Japanese handkerchief, with a string of Chinese cash. Field-Secretary Lehmann made a splendid tour through Western and Southern States.

Boston, starting with an enthusiastic celebration of Christian Endeavor's thirtieth birthday, added $23,275 to its former goodly gifts to the Building fund. The largest contribution, $15,000, was made by a Congregational trustee, Rev. James L. Hill, D. D., one of the earliest friends of the society, the man who raised the first money for Christian Endeavor at a convention, and who made a pioneer journey with Dr. Clark and Dr. Dickinson to introduce Christian Endeavor into Great Britain. An anonymous gift of $5,000 was made. Governor Foss gave $1,000. Dr. Clark's home friends in Auburndale, Mass., gave $600. Especially generous gifts were made by the officers of the United Society, Dr. Clark setting the example with great liberality.

All of these efforts advanced the Building fund more during the first half of 1911 than during five or six times that period before, so that the Atlantic City Convention in July was cheered by the news that the cash and pledges for the Building amounted to $155,021.

During the following year not much progress was made, the fund, cash and pledges, standing in June at $160,279. Gradually it rose, about a thousand dol-

Treasurer and Publication Manager Shartle.
His office is especially attractive, and he has a cordial greeting for every caller.

The United Society Book-store.
Mr. Shartle has here a most attractive display of Christian Endeavor helps of all kinds, with the newest religious books, cards, and stationery.

The United Society's Stock-room.
From this crammed-full room Christian Endeavor literature is mailed to all parts of the world.

A Corner of the Well-appointed Composing-room over Which Foreman Acker Presides.

lars a month, and by February, 1913, it was $167,361.

Finally, the Lehmann Campaign.

In April, 1914, at the outbreak of the great war, a strenuous campaign was launched for obtaining the $150,000 which was thought to be needed to complete the Building project. Secretary Lehmann was placed in charge. The sum desired was portioned out among the States, and each State was asked to give or pledge its share. Much of this campaign was generously financed by Mr. Charles G. Stewart, of Winnipeg, Manitoba.

The State unions accepted their goals loyally. Strong committees were everywhere formed to co-operate with Lehmann. Under that whirlwind leader a genuine whirlwind campaign was made from State to State. The youngest Endeavorers were invited to do their share, and Junior Builders were emphasized. Brotherly rivalry was promoted, team against team and State against State. Rallies in all parts of the country were addressed by Lehmann the indefatigable. Articles on Christian Endeavor by well-known leaders were pressed into the papers everywhere.

Secretary Lehmann continued in charge of this campaign until the fall of 1915, when he became Southern-States secretary. By that time he had received in cash $51,794, while pledges to the amount of $14,173 remained unpaid. In addition, during the year that good friend of Christian Endeavor, Mr. Jacob J. Arakelyan, had taken out an annuity of $10,000, and another friend, Mr. Louis C. Tobias, had invested $2,500 in an annuity. These sums, all put together, enabled the United Society to buy the five brick buildings on the corner of Hancock and Mt. Vernon Streets, and then, when the far better site on the corner of Mt. Vernon and Joy Streets came into the market, to use all these accumulated resources and buy that lot for $64,500, erecting on it a building costing $152,000. When the Huntington Avenue property is sold, and the property on the corner of Hancock and Mt. Vernon Streets, the United Society will own without encumbrance this fine property worth $216,500, and increasing in value every day.

The Corner-Stone Laid.

"The Otis" was purchased in January, 1917. The corner-stone of the Building was laid by Dr. Clark on July 18, 1917, after addresses by Dr. Daniel A. Poling, Dr. John F. Cowan of Hawaii, President James G. Potter of the Quebec union, Dr. James L. Hill, Mr. J. J. Arakelyan, Mr. A. J. Shartle, Hon. George W. Coleman, and Dr. Clark, with poems by John R. Clements and Amos R. Wells, and prayers by Rev. S. W. Adriance, the first Chris-

Managing Editor Wells.
His desk is the one used once by Secretary John Willis Baer.

The Christian Endeavor World Subscription Department.
Where Mr. Brown and his fine corps of assistants keep careful track of every letter and remittance.

tian Endeavor general secretary, and Prof. Carle R. Hayward, president of the Massachusetts Christian Endeavor union, the benediction being pronounced by Rev. R. P. Anderson.

The Building Dedicated.

The Headquarters Building was dedicated on July 31, 1918, in connection with sessions of the trustees of the United Society of Christian Endeavor with the field-secretaries, extending through July 30, 31, and August 1.

These meetings included a prededication prayer meeting on the evening of July 30, led by Dr. Floyd W. Tomkins, of Philadelphia. A fruitful session of the trustees occupied the morning of July 31, and in the afternoon the dedicatory services were held on the roof of the new building.

Colonel Edward H. Haskell, of the finance committee, first raised a new flag which he had presented, and the national hymn was sung. Dr. Clark presided over the services, and the opening prayer was offered by Rev. S. Winchester Adriance, the first general secretary of Christian Endeavor. Dr. Clark then pronounced the words of dedication and the vice-president of the United Society of Christian Endeavor, Dr. Howard B. Grose, offered the dedicatory prayer. The exercises closed

with the singing of the dedication hymn, written by Amos R. Wells.

On the evening of the same day the dedication rally was held in Ford Hall, Dr. Grose presiding most happily. President Woodrow Wilson sent a special letter, which was read. There were addresses by Dr. Clark; Hon. Samuel W. McCall, Governor of Massachusetts; Rev. T. Makino, vice-president of the Japan Christian Endeavor union; and General Secretary William Shaw.

August 1 was filled with profitable meetings held by the trustees and field-secretaries, and the dedication festivities closed with a banquet in Ford Hall, when 150 Endeavorers and their friends enjoyed a feast of fellowship. With Secretary Shaw as the witty toastmaster, effective addresses were made by Edward L. Sayward, one of the original members of the first Christian Endeavor society; Dr. James L. Hill, a pioneer trustee; Walter Mee, manager of the United Society's Chicago office; Dr. F. M. Sheldon, a trustee; Ex-Treasurer Hiram N. Lathrop; Rev. Robert P. Anderson, for a long time superintendent of the Builders' Union; Mrs. Francis E. Clark,—"Mother Endeavor"; Miss Grace F. Hooper, National Junior superintendent; Field-Secretary Gates, of Illinois; All-South Secretary Lehmann; Dr. William T. Johnson, a trustee; Treasurer A. J. Shartle; Field-Representative Hamilton; Fred L. Ball, of Cleveland; and President Hayward, of the Massachusetts Christian Endeavor union. Jacob J. Arakelyan, a trustee, was introduced, and two Endeavorers in khaki, Messrs. Culp and Pollock, of Pennsylvania and Massachusetts. There were letters from the first president of the United Society of Christian Endeavor, Hon. W. J. Van Patten; from the second, third, and fourth general secretaries, Dr. George M. Ward, Dr. John Willis Baer, and Dr. Von Ogden Vogt; also from Bishop Fallows, Governor Foss, and John R. Clements. And there was a poem, "The Builders of the Building," by Amos R. Wells. A prayer by Dr. Earle Wilfley, of Washington, and the benediction by Dr. Tomkins, brought the dedication services to an end.

Dr. Clark's Words of Dedication.

The two fundamental principles of Christian Endeavor are Loyalty and Fellowship, loyalty to Christ and the church, fellowship with all who love and serve the Master. Endeavorers express their loyalty in *words*, by testimony, song, and prayer; in *deeds*, by the activities of the committees and in all ways by which young people can serve their Lord and their fellow men. Their fellowship is manifested through the local, State, National, International, and World's unions, which bring together every year in conventions and union meetings literally millions of young people of all denominations.

This fellowship and these loyal and united activities have resulted not only in the formation of more than one hundred thousand church societies which have adopted Christian Endeavor principles, but in the establishment of such societies in barracks and on shipboard, in army posts and cantonments both in America and in France, in prisons and hospitals, and in many unusual places where such societies are carrying on their God-given task.

For the promotion of these principles and the enlargement of these activities this building has been erected. Toward its completion more than one hundred thousand people in almost every land have contributed.

FOR THE GLORY OF GOD THROUGH THE ESTABLISHMENT AND ENLARGEMENT OF THE LOYALTY AND FELLOWSHIP OF YOUNG CHRISTIANS IN ALL THE WORLD WE NOW DEDICATE THIS GOODLY EDIFICE IN THE NAME OF THE FATHER AND THE SON AND THE HOLY SPIRIT. AMEN.

DEDICATORY PRAYER.
By Rev. Howard B. Grose, D.D.

O Thou supreme Architect and Builder, who hast designed the universe for Thy praise and created the worlds for Thy

Associate Editor Anderson.
Our news editor, and also the versatile and accomplished Editorial Secretary of the United Society.

23

glory, we worship Thee; we acknowledge Thee in the wonder of Thy works, and praise Thee for Thy goodness to the children of men.

We thank Thee that Thou didst make man in Thine own image, the crown of Thy creation, and hast given him dominion over many things; and we praise and magnify Thy holy name that when man fell through sin, Thou didst raise him again to sonship and eternal life by the gift of Thine only begotten Son, Jesus Christ our Lord and Saviour.

We thank Thee for all those who through faith in Him have enriched the life of the world and entered into their inheritance; for all saintly lives, all holy influences, all environing forces of love and righteousness.

God of nations, our fathers' God, we thank Thee for our beloved country, and pray that Thou wilt make us and all citizens worthy of the land in which we live, true to the flag that floats above us and represents our ideals and liberties and hopes; that Thou wilt establish us as a people in righteousness so that we may be fitted for moral and spiritual leadership in the better day to be; and that Thou wilt grant unto us and our allies, who are fighting for the right, such victories as shall make possible a permanent world peace with honor and righteousness.

We thank Thee, O God, for the Christian faith, the Christian martyrs and missionaries, the Christian church—for all that Christ and His church have meant and mean to the world and to us.

We thank Thee, O God, for Christian Endeavor; for the founder to whom came this inspired idea for the spiritual development of the young people in the church of Christ; for his life and example, his inspiration to faith and service, his steady devotion to the ideals of the Master.

We thank Thee for all the loyal co-workers who with him have sought through the years to stimulate the youth of the world to love truth and seek service in a spirit of brotherhood that has broken the barriers of caste, color, and condition and girdled the earth with fraternity and good will.

We thank Thee for the world host that carries forward the Christian Endeavor banners in our own and in all lands, and beseech Thee to bless every individual life, make each faithful to pledge and purpose, strong to endure to the end; and do Thou gird with the special girding of Thy Spirit the great company of Endeavor soldier and sailor boys who

Associate Editor Kelly.
He pours a flood of light on the most difficult manuscript, and no error gets by him.

fill our service flag with stars; keep them true to manhood as to country, and make their example and influence a blessing to all who with them have responded to the nation's call.

And now especially do we thank Thee, our Father, for this day of dedication, and for this Memorial Building which we come to consecrate to Thee in the name of the Christian Endeavorers of the world.

We thank Thee for the tens of thousands of givers it represents, in all lands—givers who have built their prayers and hopes and affection into the structure, so that the stone and steel and brick are transfigured and the visible and material are glorified in the light of the invisible and spiritual.

We thank Thee for the successful completion of the work of building a house as a memorial to world Christian Endeavor, and that the loved leader in whose honor this memorial stands is with us this day. Bless him and his, O Lord, and long spare him yet to serve his day and generation; and do Thou graciously remember also all who are associated in service at headquarters or in the field, at home and abroad.

Except the Lord build the house they labor in vain that build it. Surely, Thou Master Builder, Thou hast engaged with those who have planned and perfected the work from foundation to finish; Thou hast guided the counsels of the building committee; Thou hast prospered the work of men's hands—architects, builders, and workmen; so that now we bring to Thee this completed edifice, and offer it to Thee, as a house of holiness, unto the praise and honor and glory of Thy great and holy name through the ages. Sanctify it by Thy presence; make it a perpetual source of light and leading; and grant that as pilgrim feet of old ever turned toward Jerusalem, so pilgrim Endeavorers from far and near the world over may ever come to this home centre for welcome, rest, and spiritual reinvigoration.

Be pleased to accept this building, eternal Father, in the name of Thy Son our Saviour, who hast bought us with a price, and established us among those who serve, and made us sons and heirs, even calling us friends. Behold, what manner of love the Father hath bestowed upon us. In answering love we dedicate to Thee this house not only, but ourselves, in high and holy consecration. Make this a great day in our lives, O Lord of hosts, and in the lives of all Endeavor-ers and of all Thy faithful servants everywhere. With enlarged facilities and resources give enlarged vision and purpose and power to achieve larger things for Thee in the days to come.

Our prayer is before Thee, merciful and loving Father. Hear Thou and answer graciously. Grant that this Memorial Building may stand evermore for those eternal principles of Truth, Right, Humanity, Nobility of Character, Fraternity, and Love that are finally to triumph in all the earth, and to issue in Thy good time in universal peace and good will, ushering in that glad day when every knee shall bow and every tongue confess that Christ is Lord, and He whose right it is shall reign from sea to sea.

And the glory shall be unto Thy great name, Father, Son, and Holy Spirit, now and evermore. Amen.

DEDICATION HYMN.
By Amos R. Wells.
[Tune, "Pleyel's Hymn."]

To the youth of all the earth,
To their growth in highest worth,
God to love and sin to hate,
This their home we dedicate.

To the Teacher, perfect, wise,
In whose heart all loving lies,
Master Guide to fairest fate,
This His school we dedicate.

To the living church of God
Spread through all the world abroad,
Herald of the open gate,
This its house we dedicate.

May the Father and the Son
And the Spirit, three in one,
Through the ages consecrate
This that here we dedicate.

THE BUILDERS OF THE BUILDING.
By Amos R. Wells.

Who built the Building of Christian Endeavor?
    Laid its foundations of hope and of trust,
Lifted its cornice of beauty that never
    Tempest or time shall degrade to the dust?

Not by a few was it reared in its glory;
    Thousands united its girders to raise:
Only eternity tells all the story,
    Only eternity gives all the praise.

First were the toilers of pick and of shovel,
    Artists in mortar, in brick, and in stone,
Heroes of patient and infinite trouble,
    Laboring lowly, forever unknown.

Ah, were it not for their saws and their hammers,
    Still were this building concealed in the ground;
Theirs is a language nor falters nor stammers;
    They at the Root of the matter are found.

Next is the work that defies any weigher,
　Work in ideals, in dream, and in thought,
Honor to Brainerd, to Leeds, and to Thayer!
　Hail to the vision in substance wrought!

Based on the past of an orderly science,
　Based on the past of a wonderful art,
Here are new graces, new strength and reliance,
　Here are new beauties of eye and of heart.

Who are the builders? The Building Committee,—
　Jacob, our Jacob, and this was his dream;
Shartle the faithful and Grose wise and witty,—
　Nine men in all, and a vigorous team.

Stoutly they met all the problems perplexing,
　Stoutly they batted them down to defeat,
Challenged the umpire when he was too vexing,
　Won the great game with a triumph complete.

Who are the builders? The Finance Committee,
　Peabody, Capen, who died at their post,
Bates, the beloved of the State and the city,
　Haskell the Colonel, and he is a host,

Lathrop the capable, Shartle the steady,
　Yes, and the jolly and jubilant Shaw,
Guardians of credit sagacious and ready,
　Builders of balances free from a flaw.

Who are the builders? The pleaders for money,
　Honor the beggars, a title sublime!
Poling the eloquent, Lehmann the sunny,
　Hubbell the knight of the smile and the rhyme,

Anderson, pointing his pen for a pleader,
　Shaw gayly clad in a garment of mat,
Howell the gallant, and many a leader
　Armed with shrewd argument winningly pat.

Who are the builders? The givers, the givers,
　Ah, what a host of them, near and afar!
They are the Christians, the genuine livers,
　Up where the hopes and the promises are.

Givers in India, Africa, China,
　Givers in Germany, Chile, Japan,
Canada, Boston, and North Carolina,
　Egypt, Samoa, and Afghanistan!

Givers in Britain, Australia, Dakota,
　Givers in Burma, Korea, Brazil,
Gifts from the Marshalls, Siam, Minnesota,
　Yes, and the top of them all was a Hill!

These are the builders, who built with their money,
　Glad self-denial, devotion, and grit;
Made it hilarious, really funny,
　Got a big, permanent joy out of it.

One builder more, and I need not to name him;
　Surely his building is not for the dark;
Tongues of all nations revere and acclaim him,
　Friend of the young people, Francis E. Clark!

He, in the days when the digging was hardest,
　Laid the foundation securely and deep;
God of all building! Thou surely rewardest
　All his long toiling while other men sleep.

God of all building! The builders draw near Thee,
　Lay all their tools at Thy beautiful feet,
Speak, and Thy servants shall heedfully hear Thee;
　Add Thy great word, make the building complete.

All of our labor is vain till Thou bless it,
　All of our working has missed its reward;
Here is Thy house, enter in and possess it;
　Make it forever a house of the Lord.

**The United Society Statistical Secretary
and Information Department.**

THE WHITE HOUSE
WASHINGTON

12 July, 1918.

My dear Mr. Clark:

 I have your letter of July eighth
and write to beg that upon the occasion of the
dedication of the new headquarters of the United
Society of Christian Endeavor on July thirtieth
next you will convey to those assembled my most
friendly greetings and warmest congratulations.

 In haste

   Sincerely yours,

   Woodrow Wilson

Rev. Francis E. Clark,
United Society of Christian Endeavor
Boston, Massachusetts.

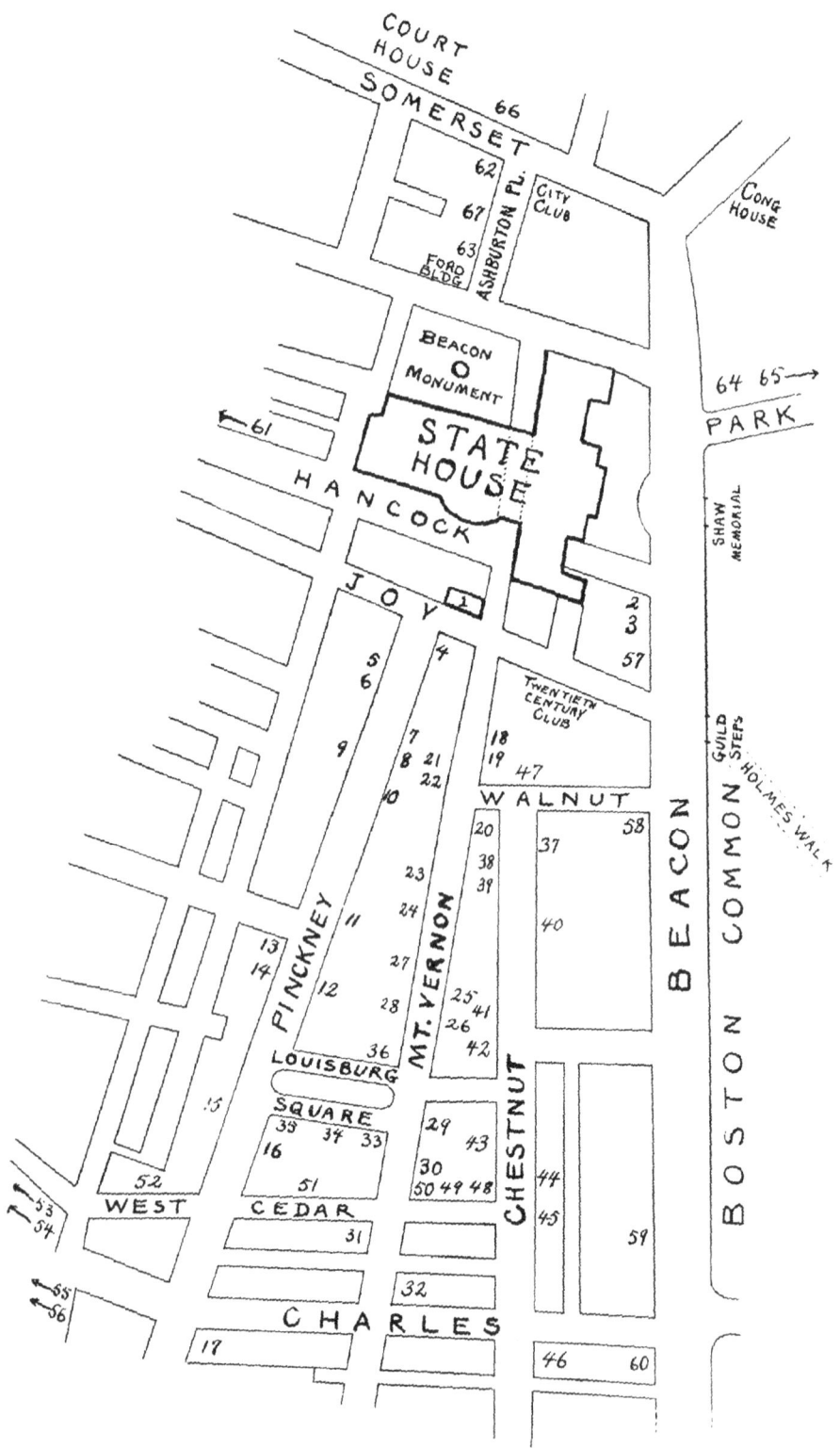

THE SURROUNDINGS OF THE BUILDING

The Christian Endeavor Building is situated on the most ancient historical site of Boston, for the first white settler of the region, the English recluse, William Blackstone, had his rude dwelling on the sunny southwestern slopes of Beacon Hill. It was Blackstone who, learning in 1630 of the trials of John Winthrop's settlement in Charlestown, so far departed from his hermit preferences as to invite the suffering little band of Puritans to come to his peninsula, especially promising them the excellent spring which flowed from Beacon Hill. Winthrop promptly accepted the invitation, and thus Boston was founded.

The early name of the place was Trimountain (retained in the modern Tremont Street), which was derived from the three summits of Beacon Hill,—Cotton Hill to the east (later Pemberton Hill), Beacon Hill in the centre (cut down with the help of the first railroad in New England), and Mt. Vernon to the west, a name perpetuated by the street which passes in front of the Christian Endeavor Building.

Mt. Vernon Street was given to the city of Boston by the famous John Hancock, Governor of Massachusetts and signer of the Declaration of Independence with bold heart and equally bold calligraphy. His pasture became the site of the present State House. Immediately in front of the new west wing of the State House was situated Hancock's home, most imposing for that day. It was surrounded by pleasant gardens, and a summer-house was situated in front of the place where our Christian Endeavor Building now is. To the north of Mt. Vernon Street were the nurseries of the Hancock estate. It is pleasant to think that the ground on which stands a building dedicated to the religious nurture of the young should first have been used for the nurture of young fruit-trees. Also to a patriotic society, which Christian Endeavor certainly is, it is inspiring to have this connection with that gallant American, John Hancock.

The Otis Building.

Our building is also associated with another famous name of Revolutionary days, that of Otis. James Otis was a noble pa-

Key to the Map.

1. Christian Endeavor Building.
2. Site of Joseph Cook's home.
3. Site of John Hancock's home.
4. Jacob Abbott (No. 4).
5. Lowell Mason (No. 9).
6. E. P. Whipple. Alice Brown (No. 11).
7. Louise Imogen Guiney (No. 16).
8. Louisa M. Alcott (No. 20).
9. Elizabeth Peabody (No. 21).
10. Edwin D. Mead (No. 30).
11. George S. Hillard (No. 54).
12. John S. Dwight (No. 66).
13. Alice Brown (No. 67).
14. Dr. and Mrs. Clark (No. 69).
15. Louisa M. Alcott (No. 81).
16. Thomas Bailey Aldrich (No. 84).
17. Celia Thaxter (No. 98).
18. Curtis Guild, Sr. (No. 26).
19. Julia Ward Howe (No. 32).
20. World Peace Foundation (No. 40).
21. Charles Francis Adams (No. 57).
22. Thomas Bailey Aldrich (No. 59).
23. Governor Claflin (Whittier) (No. 63).
24. Cornelia Warren (No. 67).
25. Boston University Theological School (72).
26. Margaret Deland (No. 76).
27. Judge Gray. Governor Long (No. 79).
28. William Ellery Channing (No. 83).
29. A. D. T. Whitney (No. 88).
30. Anne Whitney (No. 92).
31. John C. Ropes (No. 99).
32. M. A. DeWolfe Howe (No. 114).
33. W. D. Howells (No. 4).
34. Louisa M. Alcott (No. 10).
35. Jenny Lind (No. 20).
36. John G. Palfrey (No. 5).
37. George P. Lathrop (No. 8).
38. John Lothrop Motley (No. 11).
39. Julia Ward Howe (No. 13).
40. Helen Choate Prince (No. 24).
41. Edwin Booth (No. 29).
42. John G. Palfrey (No. 33).
43. Richard Henry Dana (No. 43).
44. Francis Parkman (No. 50).
45. Arlo Bates (No. 62).
46. Alice Brown (No. 96).
47. Motley. Parkman (No. 8).
48. John S. Dwight (No. 1).
49. George Lunt, T. W. Parsons, Henry C. Merwin (No. 3).
50. Percival Lowell (No. 11).
51. Edwin M. Bacon (No. 25).
52. Abbie Farwell Brown (No. 41).
53. Lucretia P. Hale (No. 127).
54. Thomas Bailey Aldrich (No. 131).
55. Site of Holmes's house (No. 164).
56. Site of James T. Fields's house (No. 148).
57. Henry Cabot Lodge (site of No. 31).
58. Wendell Phillips (No. 1, Walnut St.).
59. William H. Prescott (No. 55).
60. James Russell Lowell (No. 68).
61. Charles Sumner (No. 20).
62. Jared Sparks, etc. (No. 3).
63. Henry James (No. 13).
64. **George Ticknor, Lafayette (No. 9).**
65. Park Street Church.
66. Site of Daniel Webster's home.
67. D. L. Moody's Church.

triot whose oration against the "writs of assistance" is commemorated in one of the most spirited of the State House paintings. This oration freed the Colonists from the necessity of opening their homes to the search for smuggled goods.

The nephew of James Otis was Harrison Gray Otis, also a brilliant orator, leader with Webster of the Boston bar, third mayor of Boston, and a distinguished member of the United States Senate. He lived in a handsome house near the Christian Endeavor Building, on Beacon Street, west of Walnut Street.

His son of the same name (who died, still a young man, in 1827) married a notable woman, Eliza Henderson Bordman, who lived from 1796 to 1873. Her

Looking Down Pinckney Street to the Charles River.

home for many years was on the spot where the Christian Endeavor Building stands.

It was a stately house, famous for its brilliant social gatherings. Extended upward, it became "The Otis," a large family hotel, whose rooms of generous proportions, lofty ceilings, great mirrors, and elaborate marble and carved-wood mantelpieces maintained the grace and somewhat of the splendor of the old days. The Christian Endeavor trustees at first intended to preserve this fine old mansion, merely adapting it to our use; but it was not constructed with sufficient solidity to meet present-day building laws, and had to come down.

Other characteristics of Christian Endeavor were woven into this site by Mrs. Harrison Gray Otis, for she was an active philanthropist. Under her régime also the corner of Mt. Vernon and Joy Streets made its beginning as a literary centre, for she wrote a novel of considerable repute in its time, "The Barclays of Boston," a vivacious tale in the best-approved and most elegant style of that day.

Mrs. Otis's good works were many. Living on Mt. Vernon Street, she did much

for the fund which obtained Washington's home, Mt. Vernon, as a national possession, partly by means of a ball through which she raised $10,000. It was she who, through her influence with the State officials, brought it about that Washington's birthday became a legal holiday, and she always honored the day by giving a reception. It was also she who, in 1840, stirred up Boston women to work for the completion of Bunker Hill Monument. During four years of the Civil War she had charge of what she called a "Bank of Faith" at the Evans House (175 Tremont Street)— a place where money and supplies for the soldiers were received. Christian Endeavorers may well rejoice that their headquarters building stands on a spot so long associated with this gifted and noblehearted woman.

Quaint Pinckney Street.

One of the most interesting streets in Boston or any other city is quaint, old-fashioned Pinckney Street, which runs steeply down Beacon Hill just north of Mt. Vernon Street, around the corner from our building. The shining waters of the Charles below glorify the homely vista of brick houses, primly lined up along the narrow sidewalks.

Pinckney Street has been fairly dedicated to education and to the young. The street will always have especial interest to Christian Endeavorers because it is here, half-way down the hill at No. 69, that we find a comfortable rooming-house which Dr. and Mrs. Clark have made their home for a number of winters. Dr. Clark once wrote for THE CHRISTIAN ENDEAVOR WORLD a delightful series of sketches about "People on Our Street," which was Pinckney Street, while Mrs. Clark was so pleased with the street that she "dropped into poetry" and won a prize in the Boston Authors' Club with the following:

On little old Pinckney Street
The houses are prim and straight ;
    With hearts all a-quiver
    They gaze toward the river,
Like spinsters waiting their fate.

Like spinsters waiting their fate,
Like spinsters prim and shy,
    They stand in long rows
    On their very tiptoes,
And look up into the sky.

On little old Pinckney Street,
Those spinsters so old and wise
    Wear brick-red dresses,
    With curtains for tresses
And windows for bright little eyes

With windows for bright little eyes,
Each window a bright little eye ;
    They look over the way,
    And sadly they say,
"Alas, for the days gone by !"

No. 69.

The Pinckney Street House Where Dr. and Mrs. Clark Make Their Home.

For once on Pinckney Street
They saw writers of great renown;
They sigh for the past,
But they smile at last,
As they think of Alice Brown.

They think of Alice Brown,
And Alice Brown they greet;
For "The Children of Earth" *
Right here had their birth,
On little old Pinckney Street.

* "The Children of Earth," by Alice Brown, won a $10,000 prize.

The first notable house on Pinckney Street is No. 4, a prim little establishment where once lived Jacob Abbott, famous writer of the Rollo books and other series which did so much to open the eyes and quicken the intelligence of the boys and girls seventy-five years ago.

Louisa M. Alcott, the most popular American writer for girls, lived at No. 20, and also at No. 81 farther down the street; for the Alcotts were a poverty-stricken and migratory family.

Elizabeth Peabody, whose sister married Hawthorne and who introduced kindergarten methods into this country, kept a kindergarten at No. 21, the interesting frame house which stands with its side to the street. She helped the philosopher father of Miss Alcott, A. Bronson Alcott, in his most original school, held in the top story of the old Masonic Temple on Tremont Street, where the R. H. Stearns store is now; and she wrote a classic account of it, "Record of a School."

Thomas Bailey Aldrich once lived at No. 84, near the foot of the street, and wrote there the delightful tale of his boyhood in Portsmouth, "The Story of a Bad Boy," a book which is dear to the hearts of all boys that are worth while.

Still another man who came close to young folks was George S. Hillard, editor of the widely used Hillard Readers, who lived at No. 54, and was often visited there by his friend Hawthorne.

Celia Thaxter, who wrote much for boys and girls, spent several winters at No. 98, near the river.

If we widen the field to musical education, we shall note that Lowell Mason, the composer of noble hymns, who did so much to promote popular interest in music, lived at No. 9, while John S. Dwight, the "Brook Farmer," a notable writer on music, lived at No. 66.

Others also have lived on Pinckney Street and made it distinguished. Edwin D. Mead, publicist, author, editor, lecturer, dwelt with his brilliant wife at No. 30.

Louise Imogen Guiney, one of the most thoughtful and inspiring of American woman poets, lived at No. 16 with her mother before they removed to Oxford, England.

No. 11.

The House on Pinckney Street Where Edwin P. Whipple Lived, Now the Home of Alice Brown.

31

Edwin P. Whipple, one of the wisest of American essayists, lived at No. 11, and Mrs. Whipple continued to live there until her own death. The house was then taken by that admirable novelist, Miss Alice Brown (who once lived at No. 67), whose books now maintain most honorably the literary glory of Pinckney Street.

It is a short street; the eye takes it in at a glance from end to end; but few streets anywhere, though of many times its length, can equal this record of Pinckney Street in Boston.

Dignified Mt. Vernon Street.

Mt. Vernon Street, where Christian Endeavor has now set up its permanent abode, is a homelike yet very dignified avenue of old-fashioned residences, which is rapidly becoming, in the neighborhood of the State House, an avenue of institutions. Our neighbors toward the river are the Society for the Prevention of Cruelty to Children, the Young Men's Hebrew Association, the General Theological Library, the Massachusetts Federation of Churches, the World Peace Foundation, and the sumptuous building which houses the Theological School of Boston University.

However, as elsewhere on Beacon Hill, the literary atmosphere pervades Mt. Vernon Street. One of the most celebrated homes in Boston is the beautiful, white-pillared house, No. 59, where lived through all the closing years of his life the admired and beloved poet-novelist, Thomas Bailey Aldrich. His gracious wife lives there still. In the next house eastward, No. 57,

No. 59.   No. 57.

The Homes of Thomas Bailey Aldrich (No. 59) and of Charles Francis Adams.

lived the eminent statesman and author, Charles Francis Adams, our minister to England during the Civil War, son of one President and grandson of another.

At No. 26 lived Curtis Guild, Sr., writer of delightful books of travel, father of the Curtis Guild who was governor of Massachusetts and ambassador to Russia (in whose honor were built the Guild Steps from the Common at the beginning of Joy Street). Julia Ward Howe lived at No. 32 for three years.

In Governor Claflin's home, No. 63, was a room set apart for Whittier, and here, with the utmost freedom, the poet made his abode whenever he came to Boston (read Mrs. Claflin's "Personal Recollections of Whittier").

Cornelia Warren, novelist and philanthropist, dwelt at No. 67. Margaret Deland, the famous story-writer, lived for many years at No. 76, and built there the sunny windows for the flowers she delights to raise.

John D. Long, governor of Massachusetts and Secretary of the Navy during the Spanish-American war,—poet, historian, admirable orator, man of genial wisdom, lived for a time at No. 79, and Judge Horace Gray lived there before him.

No. 83 was the last home of the famous preacher, William Ellery Channing; see the tablet which is a part of the iron gateway. Here he died, and here lived after him his son, Dr. William Francis Channing, inventor of the electric fire-alarm telegraph.

One of the best-known writers for girls, Mrs. A. D. T. Whitney, lived at No. 88 until her marriage. Here also lived her cousin, the eccentric George Francis Train. Anne Whitney, the poet-sculptor, dwelt for many years at No. 92. Her graceful statue of Leif Ericson perpetuates her memory in Boston.

John C. Ropes, author of military histories, lived at No. 99 most of his life, and there he died. No. 114 was once the home of the biographer, M. A. DeWolfe Howe, who now lives at 26 Brimmer Street near by.

These are some of the fine associations of Mt. Vernon Street. They combine patriotism and theology, poetry, fiction, and history, science, art, and philanthropy. Mt. Vernon is a street of great memories and inspiring present-day associations. Christian Endeavor finds it good to dwell here.

Quiet Louisburg Square.

The name of Louisburg Square is a reminiscence of the great interest which Boston naturally felt in the capture of Louisburg, Cape Breton Island, by Massachusetts and other New England men in 1745. This quaint little park between Mt. Vernon and

No. 4.   In Louisburg Square.   No. 10.

No. 4 was occupied by William Dean Howells. In No. 10 Louisa M. Alcott lived, and there her father, A. Bronson Alcott, died.

Pinckney Streets, half-way down the hill, is one of the most Bostonian regions in all of old Boston. Robert Cutler brings out its characteristics charmingly in his novel, "Louisburg Square." Tradition has it that Blackstone's historic spring, whose attractions brought the first settlers from Charlestown, sprang up from the midst of the grassy plot along the centre of the square, guarded at either end by Italian statues of Columbus and Aristides, presented to the city by a Boston merchant, a Greek.

This quiet spot, which looks as if taken bodily from some out-of-the-way corner of London, has its full share of the bookish memories of Beacon Hill. No. 4 was one of the numerous homes in Boston and Cambridge that were occupied by William Dean Howells, the present "dean" of American letters. Palfrey the historian removed from Chestnut Street to No. 5 Louisburg Square. No. 10 was the last home of Louisa M. Alcott. Here she lived from 1885 till her death in 1888. She did not die in this house, but in Roxbury; but her philosopher father, A. Bronson Alcott, made the house his home at the close of his life, and here he died.

No. 20, at the northwest corner of the square, is pleasantly associated with the sweet singer, Jenny Lind; for it was in this house that she married the conductor of her American tour, Otto Goldschmidt.

Charming Chestnut Street.

Chestnut Street, which runs down the hill between Mt. Vernon Street and Beacon Street, may well be called the Street of Historians. Certainly no other street in

America has been the dwelling-place of so many eminent writers of history.

John Lothrop Motley, the brilliant author of "The Rise of the Dutch Republic" and other Dutch histories, lived at the dignified house, No. 11. When a boy he lived at the head of the street, at No. 7 (probably now No. 8) Walnut Street; and in the garret of this house he often played with his childhood friend, Wendell Phillips.

No. 50.

Home of Francis Parkman.

33

The Homes of Julia Ward Howe (on the left) and of John Lothrop Motley (on the right).

In this same house, No. 8 Walnut Street, Francis Parkman lived for eight years; but for nearly thirty years, till the end of his life, this great writer on pioneer days in the United States and Canada lived at No. 50 Chestnut Street, half-way down the hill. The exceedingly gloomy aspect of this severely plain residence may be said to symbolize the tragedy of Parkman's life of suffering, while the exceedingly cheerful air of Chestnut Street itself may typify Parkman's invincible courage which surmounted all obstacles and gave us histories of heroism all a-tingle with the spirit of freedom and romance.

A close neighbor to Parkman's house, though on Beacon Street, lived William H. Prescott, historian of the conquest of Mexico and Peru, a man whose physical misfortune, his lifelong battle with blindness, remind us of the struggles of Parkman, while his splendid optimism, and the glorious swing of his books, are akin to the spirit and the works of Motley and Parkman.

Add John G. Palfrey, the historian of New England, who lived at No. 33, and you have credited this portion of Beacon Hill with an unexcelled galaxy of historical writers.

But this is by no means all the glory of Chestnut Street. In the somewhat stately house, No. 8, at the top of the hill, lived the poet-novelist, George Parsons Lathrop,

with his poet wife, Rose Hawthorne Lathrop, daughter of Nathaniel Hawthorne. Julia Ward Howe, author of "The Battle-Hymn of the Republic" and eminent in many good works, lived for a time at No. 13. Helen Choate Prince, the novelist, granddaughter of Rufus Choate, lived at No. 24.

Once Edwin Booth, the great Shakespearean actor, dwelt in the unique home, No. 29, and gave dramatic readings in the large private hall which may be seen back of the little green court between the house and the beautiful new chapel of the Theological School of Boston University.

Richard Henry Dana lived at No. 43; Arlo Bates, poet, novelist, and teacher, occupied No. 62; Miss Alice Brown once lived at No. 96. All these, with other celebrities of only a little less extended fame, render Chestnut Street one of the most interesting and notable of thoroughfares.

Other Famous Streets.

West Cedar Street runs along the western slope of the hill, below Louisburg Square. No. 1 was the home until his death of the musician, John S. Dwight, and is the present home of the Harvard Musical Association,—a house with a most interesting interior and many delightful associations with authors and musicians. George Lunt, the charming essayist, lived in No. 3. Here also lived Dr. T. W. Parsons, whose poems are Grecian in their fine quality and wise simplicity and clearness.

The Home of Edwin Booth.
A glimpse of the heavily shaded courtyard, of the pillared entrance, and, in the rear, of the assembly hall.

34

G. P. Lathrop's Home (on the right).

Henry C. Merwin, the well-known biographer and essayist, has also lived in this notable home.

At No. 11 lived the famous astronomer, noted for his studies of the canals of Mars, Percival Lowell. Edwin M. Bacon, the leading writer on old Boston, dwelt for nearly twenty years at No. 25, then removing to 16 Pinckney Street. Miss Abbie Farwell Brown, whose wise and witty writings for children, in prose and verse, are widely read, lives at No. 41.

Charles Street, running along the western base of Beacon Hill, must serve as the limit of our survey. Among the most interesting houses here are No. 127, where lived Lucretia P. Hale, the sister of Edward Everett Hale, author of the immortal "Peterkin Papers"; and No. 131, where Aldrich lived for the ten years during which he wrote "Marjorie Daw," "Cloth of Gold," "Prudence Palfrey," "Flower and Thorn," "Miss Mehetabel's Son," "A Rivermouth Romance," "A Midnight Fantasy," "The Queen of Sheba," and "The Stillwater Tragedy."

On the opposite side of the street stood until recently two other notable dwellings, No. 164, where Holmes lived and where he wrote "The Professor at the Breakfast-table," "The Guardian Angel," "Elsie Venner," and "Dorothy Q"; and No. 148, where James T. Fields, the author and publisher, lived and died, and where he entertained many of the leading British and American writers of his day. Here, for many years after his death, his wife, Mrs. Annie Fields, essayist and poet, continued to live with her friend the novelist, Sarah Orne Jewett.

Boston's Own Beacon Street.

Beacon Street, in the portion that bounds Beacon Hill on the south, is full of interest. No. 10½ is the stately home of the Athe-

naeum, one of the oldest libraries in America, founded in 1807. Among its founders was Emerson's father, and it is especially rich in Americana, including the library of George Washington.

In front of the new western wing of the State House was until recently a plain brick house rendered notable by the occupancy of Joseph Cook, the philosopher, whose "Monday lectureship" in Park Street Church was so famous. Next on the west is the site of John Hancock's mansion, the destruction of which was so deplorable. At No. 31 (also now torn down) Henry Cabot Lodge, statesman and author, used to live while in Boston.

The large square brick house at the corner of Walnut Street (No. 1 Walnut Street) was the first brick house on Beacon Street, and was considered when it was built to be far out of town! It was the home of John Phillips, the first mayor of Boston. Here his famous son, Wendell Phillips, was born, and here the inspiring orator lived until his marriage with his beloved wife,—a marriage very distasteful to the first mayor of Boston.

No. 55, the sunny house near the foot of the hill, was the home of William Hickling Prescott during the last two decades of his life. Here he wrote "The Conquest of Peru" and "Philip the Second," and here, in a top-floor study at the back of the house carefully guarded with curtains, the gallant historian groped his way through the darkness to those shining chapters in which the dead past lives again.

The Birthplace of Wendell Phillips.
Built by his father, the first mayor of Boston. The orator lived here till his marriage.

Lowell spent many months at No. 68, visiting his sister, Mrs. S. R. Putnam. This is also the street where Oliver Wendell Holmes and Julia Ward Howe lived during their closing decades, but their homes were farther west, well beyond the neighborhood of Beacon Hill.

Sumner and Others.

The other streets of Beacon Hill are not so rich in precious associations, though all of them have their fine memories. On Hancock Street, at No. 20 near the foot of the hill, lived for many years the great anti-slavery orator, Charles Sumner. The tablet on the house bears witness to this historic occupancy.

The short Ashburton Place to the east was for a time the home (at No. 13) of Henry James and Henry James, Jr., while at No. 3 was a boarding-house whose distinguished patrons were Jared Sparks the historian, Horace Mann the educator, and the three Peabody sisters, Mary who became Mrs. Horace Mann, Sophia who became Mrs. Nathaniel Hawthorne, and Elizabeth the pioneer kindergartner.

A Great Little Street.

Park Street, a short thoroughfare reaching up the hill from the south, counts great associations with every building.

Park Street Church at the corner had once for its popular pastor, William Henry Harrison Murray ("Adirondack" Murray), editor of THE CHRISTIAN ENDEAVOR

Charles Sumner's Home (in the centre)

WORLD in the old *Golden Rule* days before Dr. Clark and his associates bought it for Christian Endeavor. He was most famous for his sprightly sketches and tales of outdoor life, which really introduced the Adirondacks to the American people, and started the healthy present-day fondness for vacations in the open. The present pastor of this church is Rev. A. Z. Conrad, D. D., who organized the first Intermediate Society of Christian Endeavor.

No. 2 Park Street was Motley's last home in Boston before he went to England as United States Minister. Josiah Quincy, the distinguished second mayor of Boston, occupied No. 4, and his father of the same name, who was for many years president of Harvard, lived at No. 5. Both of these wrote books.

No. 4 is the home of the great publishing house of Houghton Mifflin Company, whose list comprises the works of most of the leading American authors. Here also *The Atlantic Monthly* was published for many years until its removal to the Christian Endeavor Building.

No. 8, the Union Club, has seen as club occupants many of Boston's most famous sons; it is the former home of Abbott Lawrence, one of the most honored of Bostonians.

George Ticknor, historian of Spanish literature, lived in No. 9 at the corner, and there Lafayette stayed during his visit to Boston in 1824.

The Beacon.

The summit of Beacon Hill was formerly called Centry Hill; it is the watch-hill of Boston. The famous beacon on a tall mast based on a stone foundation was an iron crane sixty-five feet above the top of the hill, on which a barrel of tar might be hung, or some other flaming signal, visible far inland in case of hostile invasion. A watchman was stationed near it, who could ascend the mast on spikes driven into it.

On November, 1789, the ancient beacon (it was first set up in 1634) blew down, and the next year a brick monument sixty feet high was erected in its place. It was designed by Bulfinch, and bore a large wooden gilded eagle, while the pedestal was distinguished by eloquent inscriptions, written by the architect himself, commemorating the events of the Revolution.

The present monument northeast of the State House is a stone duplicate of Bulfinch's, though of course on much lower ground, and carries at the base the original slate tablets from the old brick monument, which was taken down when the hill was levelled in 1811. This monument, therefore, is an epitome of the history of Boston.

The portion of Beacon Hill occupied by the State House was, as has already been

No. 55.

Home of William H. Prescott.

said, John Hancock's cow-pasture. The making of rope was a prominent industry of Boston in the old seafaring days, and both Hancock Street, west of the State House, and Joy Street next to Hancock Street, are along the course of these ancient rope-walks.

Joy Street, which bounds our Christian Endeavor Building on the west, is named from Dr. John Joy, an apothecary of the old days, who owned the estate west of Hancock's. He built a wooden house on it, much against the will of his wife, who objected to living so far out of town! This Joy estate was east of the great estate of twenty acres owned by Copley, the famous portrait painter,—an estate reaching to the water, and including Blackstone's pioneer possessions. Copley lived and worked where now stands the fine stone building of the Somerset Club, 42 Beacon Street. When the artist left this country for England he sold this princely estate for $18,550! Harrison Gray Otis was one of the purchasers, and Dr. Joy was another.

An Institutional Centre.

Beacon Hill is the home of many institutions of great influence and wide interest. Near our building, on Joy Street, is the Twentieth Century Club, famous for its Saturday discussion lunches. Another neighbor on Joy Street is the Diocesan House of the Episcopal Church, while near by on Beacon Street are the Congregational House and the Unitarian Building, centres of those denominations. On the other side of the State House is Ford Hall, the Baptist centre, where our Christian Endeavor trustee, Dr. Grose, edits *Missions*, and our other Baptist trustee, Hon. George W.

Coleman, conducts that splendid social experiment, the Ford Hall Forum. The Methodist headquarters are not far from Beacon Hill, in Copley Square.

Webster and Others.

Many of the interesting bits of Beacon Hill history can be referred to only briefly. The Revere House, at the foot of the hill on the north, was the temporary abode of the Prince of Wales in 1860, of Grant, Sherman, Sheridan, and Dom Pedro, while Daniel Webster made it his customary stopping-place. The great orator's first home in Boston was on Beacon Hill, and was where the Court House now stands, east of the State House.

Ashburton Place, connecting the Court House and the State House, contains two notable buildings besides Ford Hall, already mentioned. One is the spacious and beautiful Boston City Club, housing the largest club in the country. The other is the substantial stone edifice which is now the Law School of the Boston University, but which was formerly the Mount Vernon Congregational Church, where D. L. Moody was converted and began his glorious life of Christian service.

The State House.

The State House—at least, the central portion in front, was the work of Charles Bulfinch, who was also the architect of the National Capitol. The corner-stone was drawn up the steep hill in 1795 by fifteen white horses, representing the States then in the Union. It was laid by the Masons, Paul Revere being the grand master, and the address was made by Samuel Adams, then governor.

37

During recent years this ancient building has received extensive additions toward the north, east, and west, so that it is now of many times the original size, but the old walls and rooms have been wisely retained.

The interior of the State House has much of profound interest, including Memorial Hall with its relics of the Civil War, Doric Hall with its story of the Revolution, the chastely beautiful Senate Chamber (formerly the Hall of Representatives) with its memories of the great orators of Massachusetts, the new Hall of Representatives with its wonderful frieze bearing the names of eminent citizens of Massachusetts, the State Library with the priceless journal of Governor William Bradford—the so-called "log of the Mayflower," the Senate reception-room so full of historic memorials, the fine paintings of historic scenes and the many noble statues. Among the latter, in front of the State House, is a statue of Webster by Hiram Powers (Edward Everett gave the dedicatory address), one of Horace Mann (the gift of Massachusetts school children and teachers), and the spirited equestrian statue of General Hooker. From the gilded dome of the State House, accessible to visitors in ordinary times, the country and ocean are to be seen for many miles in all directions.

Here we conclude our survey of Beacon Hill. Surely it would be difficult to find anywhere a site so suitable for the world centre of Christian Endeavor. Beacon Hill is an eminence consecrated to all that is noblest in American life, its patriotism, its literature, its education, its philanthropy, its religion. May Christian Endeavor be worthy of these surroundings, and do much during coming years to add to their glory.

www.ingramcontent.com/pod-product-compliance
Lightning Source LLC
Chambersburg PA
CBHW030310030426
42337CB00012B/655